RESTORED
Moments

A SIX-DAY GRIEF DEVOTIONAL

MARILYN WILLIS, MA, LPCC, NCC

For my
Lord and Savior, Jesus Christ
"Let us hold unswervingly to the hope we
profess, for he who promised is faithful."
Hebrews 10:23

Need a speaker for your event?
Contact Marilyn at the website below.

Restored Moments: A Six-Day Grief Devotional

**For free resources and more visit
www.GoodMourningWithMarilyn.com.**

TABLE OF CONTENTS

Welcome to His Restoration

Welcome
to His Restoration

After losing a loved one, if you find yourself in chaos, suffering, in turmoil, confused, lost, brokenhearted, and in need of Jesus' restoration, then you are in the right place. God has not forgotten you.

When many of us hear the word restored, we think of furniture or home restoration. When you restore a piece of furniture, that item's original structure or foundation remains. However certain aspects of the item that are rusted, broken, or no longer desired must be torn down, rebuilt, or refreshed. "The same process is true when it comes to loss. Grief changes more than it ends. Though loss never disappears, it can be healed, and your life can be restored. As a survivor of loss, we are like a beat-up piece of furniture that needs to be refurbished, our foundation is still the same, but our body, mind, and spirit must be renewed and restored" (RESTORED, 2020).

Here in this "RESTORED" devotional series, as you commit yourself to Christ, may He guide you along unfamiliar paths (Psalm 10:14, Isaiah 42:16). As you thirst for Him in a dry and parched land of sorrow, may He give you streams of living water. As your body longs for Him in physical exhaustion, may He restore it with His rest and abundant life (Psalm 63, Isaiah 55, John 6:35, Matthew 11:28).

It is my great honor to write this devotional for you, my brothers and sisters in Christ. When I wrote the workbook "RESTORED," I said that I feel God has something special, deeper healing, for His children. You will discover this deeper healing as we apply the 5 "RESTORED" Principles: Reestablish Order, Reset Expectations, Remember Your Loved One, Renew Identity, and Restore Life After Loss. In the workbook, these principles serve as a map to guide each person in their unique grief journey through the critical challenges that loss presents. During this devotional, you and I will need God's help and restoration in the same 5 critical areas.

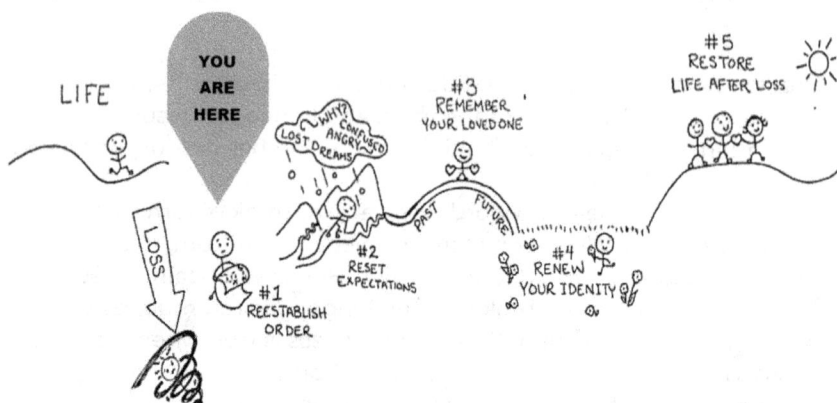

May the Lord turn your darkness into light before you and make your rough places smooth (Isaiah 42:16). May God give you His strength to be strong and courageous, not afraid or discouraged. Thank you, Father, that you are with us wherever we go, even into the depths of grief (Joshua 1:9).

You are our God of Order, our God of Comfort, our God of Memory, our God of Renewal, and our God of Restoration!

Today, may we discover your restored moment. Amen.

DAY ❶

GOD OF ORDER
Reestablish
My Order

Day 1

Has grief brought chaos to your life?
Do your days seem out of control?
Is your body in constant instability?

As you navigate loss,
your first need is for order.

Picture yourself standing in front of a worn, unstable chair that needs refurbishing. How can this chair be made effective for use again? First, the chair needs a secure, stable, and safe foundation. Perhaps this means bracing wobbly legs or gluing broken ones. Likewise, to navigate loss we must create a firm footing in ourselves by reestablishing order. Only then can we do the difficult work of accepting the reality of our loss and mourning.

God of Order

God orders all things and can be trusted with even our biggest trials! Let us take a small look at the many things God has ordered around us.

- Trees transport water from roots through their trunk to leaves through molecules climbing up the tree one by one, like blocks constructing a building.

- Water falls from the sky to the ground, flows through streams to rivers to lakes to oceans then evaporates to form clouds and then the process starts over again.

- Our whole solar system orbits and moves seamlessly, gravity holding each planet in its place. If that is not enough, we are held to earth due to this same gravity!

- Somehow the sun is exactly far enough away that it does not burn up our planet and yet close enough to provide us with the energy that is needed for all life here on earth.

"The breath of God produces ice, and the broad waters become frozen. He loads the clouds with moisture; he scatters his lightning through them. At his direction they swirl around over the face of the whole earth to do whatever he commands them." Job 37:10-12

"Lift up your eyes and look to the heavens: Who created all these? He who brings out the starry host one by one and calls forth each of them by name. Because of his great power and mighty strength, not one of them is missing." Isaiah 40:26

- Our human bodies are composed of many types of cells, each one serving a specific function. From bone cells that hold us upright, to skin cells to protect our body, to blood cells that transport oxygen and nutrients.

- Our brain's neurotransmitters can control every aspect of our bodies depending on what part of the brain is activated.

> *"For you created my inmost being; you knit me together in my mother's womb."*
> *Psalm 139:13*

God has created order for our entire world including plants, water, the solar system, the weather, our bodies, and more! Part of trusting our God of order is reflecting on who He is. The Bible tells us that Christ is our chief cornerstone holding up our house's foundation (Ephesians 2:20) (1 Peter 2:6).

> *"So this is what the Sovereign Lord says: 'See, I lay a stone in Zion, a tested stone, a precious cornerstone for a sure foundation; the one who relies on it will never be stricken with panic.'"*
> *Isaiah 28:16*

✍ Marilyn's Reflections

I love order. Those that know me know that there is truly a place for everything and everything must be in its place. Schedules, lists, categories, and tables are where I thrive. So, what happens when things start to get out of place? At first, I try to be ok with a few little piles. As the piles in a corner turn into a room-sized mess and the mess spills from rooms into my whole house, something cracks inside of me. I become a woman with a mission. My husband warns the children that Mom needs a moment. I start dashing in and out of rooms throwing items into their areas and throwing away anything that seems to not have a purpose. Why do I go a little bit crazy when I see too much disorder? Because there is a connection between our physical environment and our mental well-being. A disordered house can be a sign of a disordered spirit, or unintended disorder can quickly work to discourage and fatigue our soul. The chaos that has taken root in my mind has now become a physical reality.

During loss, grief disrupts the most basic of our activities. Routines no longer give our days structure and showers no longer keep our bodies clean. Inwardly the piles turn into mounds of unspoken words and sorrows. We truly are wasting away...and for what purpose? Why are these internal messes accumulating and what are we to do with the chaos?

> A disordered house can be a sign of a disordered spirit.

James 1:2-7 addresses our chaos head-on. James tells us that our trials are sanctifying us, making us more like Christ. We are not to suffer on our own, though. During this sanctification process, which requires faith and perseverance, we are to ask God for help! James goes on to say that when we ask for help, we must not doubt. When confronted with piles in my home, I can honestly say that may faith in God's control is not at the front of my mind. Likewise, when my mom died, doubt wreaked havoc in my heart and mind. What are we to do when we feel tossed like a "wave of the sea blown and tossed by the wind"? Invite the God of order to reestablish order in your heart and mind so you can have a firm footing from which to begin your grief journey (Isaiah 26:3).

> *"You will keep in perfect peace those whose minds are steadfast, because they trust in you."*
> *Isaiah 26:3*

During loss, we need to reestablish the order of our daily lives by taking care of our basic needs, which include things such as shelter, safety, sleeping, exercise, eating, and routine. However, let us not neglect our greatest source of restoration: faith, perseverance, and hope in our cornerstone, our foundation, Christ.

Lord, we need you. I think of Job and his great suffering. Just as you had mercy on Job, may your face shine upon us as we seek you. Please reveal to each of us how you are The God of order. Please create an order for each of us in our hearts and minds. May we each be able to cry in our own hearts these words penned by Job, "Though He slay me, yet will I trust Him." Job 13:15
Amen.

♫ Find a Spotify Music Playlist for God of Order at this link: www.goodmourningwithmarilyn.com/day1

Application

In Psalm 19:1-6, what words stand out to you about our "God of Order"?

In Psalm 19:7-10, what words stand out to you about how connecting with God creates order in your heart and mind?

From Hebrews 10:22-25, what are some ways you can bring order to the chaos of grief right now?

Step out in faith and ask God for His guidance in this area.

DAY 2

GOD OF COMFORT
Reset
My Expectations

Day 2

? In your grief are you experiencing yearning, longing, disbelief, extreme sadness, confusion, numbness, overwhelm, exhaustion, insomnia, anger, inability to focus, agitation, or anxiety? Do you feel you have lost a part of yourself?

As you navigate loss,
your second need is for comfort.

Our chair's foundation is now secure, but it is full of splinters making it uncomfortable to sit on. Splinters need sanding; rough edges require some material removed creating smooth curves. Navigating loss requires us to reset expectations in our hearts and minds. As we encounter feelings, thoughts, and questions we must learn to confront, express, and release them. Now we have a smooth surface to journey forward.

God of Comfort

We all expect certain outcomes in life. After investing time in a college education, we expect a job to follow. Spending a significant amount of time in a dating relationship often carries the assumption of marriage and a love-filled relationship. Expecting mothers dream of the day pregnancies produce a new life that we'll hold and cherish. It is when these hopes and dreams are turned on their head that an extreme physical, emotional, and spiritual reaction occurs. We call this reaction grief. We need God to restore our comfort and hope.

One size does not fit all when it comes to comfort in shoes or in your loss. Together we will discover five ways to find comfort through the stories of David, Job, Jeremiah, Jesus, and the Acts church body. As we grapple with their stories, we gain insight into ways God restores our own comfort.

Way #1 God Restores Comfort: Expressing Grief Emotions

God restores comfort and peace through the action of expressing grief emotions, casting your cares on God. He then will bring His comfort, sustain you and never let you be shaken (Psalm 55:22) (Philippians 4:6-7). Do not be afraid to tell God how you are feeling. We must cast our cares on the Lord if we want Him to carry us through them (Psalm 55:22).

> "Cast your cares on the Lord and he will sustain you; he will never let the righteous be shaken."
> (Psalm 55:22)

- In Psalm 42, David does not bottle up his emotions or avoid them instead he cries out in the Psalms when his soul is downcast (Psalm 42:5-11).

Way #2 God Restores Comfort: Trusting in God's Goodness

God restores comfort and peace through trusting in His goodness and giving thanks for everything. Even when our circumstances do not change, in time these prayers of thanksgiving supernaturally uplift our spirits.

"The Lord gave and the Lord has taken away; may the name of the Lord be praised."
(Job 1:20)

- Job suffers many losses. Job cries out for mercy and then he sings with praise. He never loses sight of God's faithfulness (Job 1:18-22).

Way #3 God Restores Comfort: Music that Soothes

God restores comfort and peace through music. There are countless stories in the Bible where people express their sadness through song.

"Restore us to yourself, Lord, that we may return; renew our days as of old..."
(Lamentations 5:21)

Allow music to comfort your soul when you cannot sleep and when you cannot rise. God hears these cries. Through their songs both Jeremiah and David are reminded of God's compassion.

- Jeremiah writes the entire book of Lamentations in the style of ancient Jewish funeral songs or chants. In these Laments, Jeremiah pours out his grief, and glimpses of hope emerge.
- David uses music throughout the Psalms to ask God to uplift his downcast spirit.

By day the Lord directs his love, at night his song is with me—
a prayer to the God of my life.
(Psalm 42:8)

Way #4 God Restores Comfort:
Faithful Prayers

God restores joy and wisdom through our faithful prayers that are spoken in trust (John 16:24) (Romans 12:12) (James 1:5). God causes these prayers to overflow into a new hope.

- Jesus cries out to His Father when He does not feel able to bear anymore and He asks God to "take this cup from me" (Luke 22:42).

  Jesus does not allow Himself to make decisions based on what He knows He must endure on the cross. Instead, He prays and refocuses His mind on God. These same prayers are then used by God to overflow into hope (Romans 15:13) (Hebrews 10:23). Although God does not take away Jesus' trial of going to the cross, God answers His prayers by sending an angel to give Him strength!

"An angel from heaven appeared to him and strengthened him."
(Luke 22:43)

Way #5 God Restores Comfort:
Other People

God sustains us through each other! We need each other, especially when the world's troubles arise.

- God calls believers to be His hands and feet for each other. Just look at the church in the book of Acts who were noted for: fellowship, prayer, meals, sincere hearts, worship time, and the giving of resources for one another (Acts 2).

"They devoted themselves to the apostles' teaching and to fellowship, to the breaking of bread and to prayer. Everyone was filled with awe at the many wonders and signs performed by the apostles. All the believers were together and had everything in common. They sold property and possessions to give to anyone who had need. Every day they continued to meet together in the temple courts. They broke bread in their homes and ate together with glad and sincere hearts, praising God and enjoying the favor of all the people. And the Lord added to their number daily those who were being saved." (Acts 2:42-47)

There are countless other examples of ways God provides comfort throughout the Bible.

Each of these examples is a reminder that we have a savior who cares deeply about our troubles and will meet us in our weakest moments. Jesus' entire ministry was about showing up, loving people where they are at, and being an example of how to care for one another. In John 14:27, Jesus left His disciples with these words and He leaves them with us too...

"Peace I leave with you; my peace I give you. I do not give to you as the world gives. Do not let your hearts be troubled and do not be afraid." (John 14:27)

✍ Marilyn's Reflections

Comfort is so needed throughout our lives. I think of a friend who recently lost all she owned in a fire. And another who lost their father to disease. I think of war-torn countries and the poor praying and waiting for a way to obtain their next meal. I think of the elderly left isolated and alone. So many are hurting. We truly live in a world full of troubles and tribulations. I am so grateful that Jesus gives us this promise in John 16:33, "I have told you these things, so that in me you may have peace. In this world you will have trouble. But take heart! I have overcome the world" (John 16:33).

But how do you "take heart?" How can you overcome your troubles?

In Exodus 3, God sees His people in need of comfort as they suffer the hardship of being Pharaoh's slaves. God reveals Himself through the burning bush. Moses wonders why the bush does not look burnt. He goes to inspect it and then God says, "Take off your sandals, for the place where you are standing is holy ground" (Exodus 3:5). There is no better way to describe God's comfort than each of us entering His holy ground. Like Moses and the burning bush, these gifts of mercy allow the Lord's goodness to dwell among us.

> His comfort almost always shows up in ways we would never expect.

When I was fifteen, before my mom was diagnosed with cancer, my parents were contemplating buying a new house. They took me to look at it one last time. When we got there, worms covered the floor. They were along the wall of every room! We examined the house and could not figure out where they came from. I would have thought I somehow invented this memory if my dad did not also remember this worm invasion. One thing we knew for sure, this house has a problem with keeping unwanted bugs out. And we also took this as a warning. That visit did not end with a house sale.

A year later my mom was diagnosed with stage 4 ovarian cancer. Because of remaining in our current home, we also remained in a strong community instead of uprooting during a time when we desperately needed our neighbors. They were our comfort, God's hands and feet, during the three-year period when mom was sick. Here are my dad's words describing these neighbors, "A hundred different ways they came, meals were delivered, family and friends stayed at our house with the kids while I was at the hospital with Shirley. They chauffeured Shirley to medical appointments and to dialysis treatments, they did our laundry and they shuttled the kids to their school, band, and sporting events" (RESTORED, 2020). These faithful friends helped us survive. I believe this was God's gift of mercy for my family.

His comfort almost always shows up in ways we would never expect.

During loss, we need to reset our expectations by seeking God's comfort and asking Him to open our eyes to His gifts of mercy.

Like Moses, may you enter God's holy ground, dwell in His goodness, and see His mercy.

Like David, may you pour out your emotions to the Lord and allow Him to sustain you.

Like Job, may you never lose sight of God's faithfulness.

Like Jeremiah, may you use music to comfort your soul.

Like Jesus, may you pray and allow God to strengthen you during the storm.

Like in the book of Acts, may you allow your brothers and sisters in Christ to support you.

Lord, we are suffering. Our hearts are faint within us. Come, Lord Jesus, bring your comfort into our hearts full of sorrow (Jeremiah 8:18). May we each be able to cry in our own hearts these words penned by David, "Why, my soul, are you downcast? Why so disturbed within me? Put your hope in God, for I will yet praise him, my Savior and my God" (Psalm 42:5).
Amen.

♫♪ Find a Spotify Music Playlist for God of Comfort at
this link: www.goodmourningwithmarilyn.com/day2

Application

Read David's words in Psalm 55:22, what cares do you have that you have yet to cast onto the Lord? As you tell God about these cares, what comfort arises in you?

Read Job 1:20-21, what was Job's reaction to loss? What would it look like to praise God in your grief? As you praise God in your grief, what thoughts arise for you about God?

Is there a certain song that brings you comfort? Listen to this today.

Read John 16:24, write out a way you need God's strength right now. Pray and ask for His help in this area.

Is there a family member, friend, neighbor, or even a stranger that God has used in your life? Who is one person you could reach out to for support?

DAY ❸

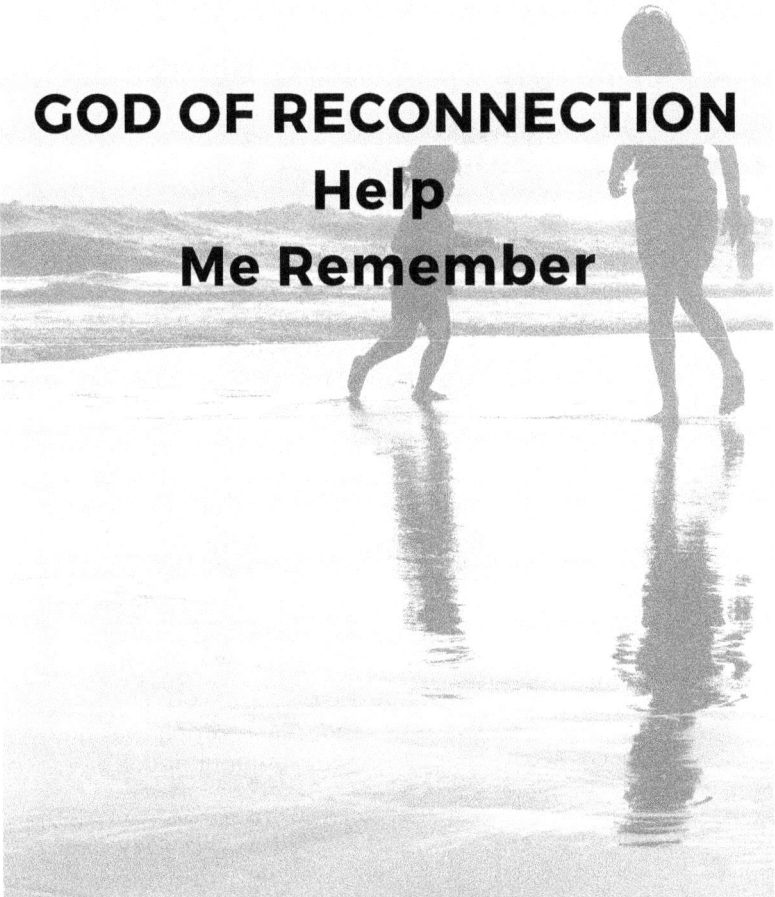

GOD OF RECONNECTION
Help
Me Remember

$\mathcal{D}ay\ 3$

? **Will my memories cause sadness to take over? How can they provide joy?**

As you navigate loss, your third need is hope through reconnection.

Our chair is now safe and smooth. Continued restoration requires preparing the chair for paint with a coat of primer. To navigate loss, reconnect to God's promises and memories of His past faithfulness in your life. Also, remember your loved one by honoring them and your relationship with them through intentional acts of remembrance. Memories are the bridge between your past and your future. They put the puzzle pieces of your life back together and, like a primer, seal in and protect your foundation.

God of Reconnection

The entire Bible is story after story of reconnecting to God's faithfulness. A great example of how God calls us to continually reconnect with Him through our memories of His past faithfulness is found in the book of Joshua. Joshua 4 says, the Israelites witness God's miracle as he parts the Jordan River to bring them safely across.

God says, 'Tell them to take up twelve stones from the middle of the Jordan, from right where the priests are standing, and carry them over with you and put them down at the place where you stay tonight... These stones are to be a memorial to the people of Israel forever' (Joshua 4:3, 7).

A memorial is "something designed to preserve the memory of a person, event, commemorative of or relating to the memory" (Dictionary.com, 2018).

"He said to the Israelites, 'In the future when your descendants ask their parents, 'What do these stones mean?' tell them, 'Israel crossed the Jordan on dry ground...
He did this so that all the peoples of the earth might know that the hand of the Lord is powerful and so that you might always fear the Lord your God.'"
(Joshua 4:21-22, 24)

The Israelites took twelve stones to remember that God provided. When we begin a new journey, we preserve important moments in life with a memorial so that we never forget the amazing things the Lord has done for us. For completing school it's a certificate, for a birthday it's a party, for a holiday it's a celebration.

For your loved one, this will be a celebration that reminds you of who they were and whom you want to be because of them." (excerpt from RESTORED Workbook, 2020).

For your relationship with Christ, this will be remembering who He is and the ways He has been faithful in your life.

✍ Marilyn's Reflections

"Abby put on your shoes." "Isaiah have you used the potty?" "It is time to go outside, can you hear me?" Those of us that are blessed to be parents of young children hear ourselves ask such questions day in and day out. We give and give, train, love, and hope for our children. As I repeat myself for the twentieth time, I do get frustrated. As I reflect on the life of a parent one thing becomes very clear to me: my job is to help my children remember. Remember how to be safe. Remember what they should be doing. Remember their manners and numbers. Hopefully, as they grow, the main thing they remember is that they belong. Home is fortified through the memories made, the safe place and training given, and the love received. Home helps us to grow so we may reach our full potential (Proverbs 22:6) (1 Corinthians 11:1).

When I look at myself as God's child and I reflect on how many times I repeat myself as a parent, I feel very small. Thank goodness, like a mother with her children, our gracious God helps us remember. Commands are God's way of saying "My daughter Marilyn, remember!" I am SO grateful that as I remember God's truth, He never stops reminding me not to fall into that old sin, to keep my focus on Him, and that I belong to Him (John 14:26).

99

Jesus is calling to you too,
'My Child,
Remember!'

66

Jesus is calling to you too, "My child, remember!" We must keep His words on our hearts, meditating and teaching our minds with them, always be talking about them, and have reminders of them wherever we look (Deuteronomy 6:4-8). It is through this repetition that we are building the ability to recall these truths during our trials! We all need ways to remember Him throughout our days and years.

"Hear, O Israel: The Lord our God, the Lord is one. Love the Lord your God with all your heart and with all your soul and with all your strength. These commandments that I give you today are to be on your hearts. Impress them on your children. Talk about them when you sit at home and when you walk along the road, when you lie down and when you get up. Tie them as symbols on your hands and bind them on your foreheads. Write them on the doorframes of your houses and on your gates." (Deuteronomy 6:4-8)

This past January, I was encouraged by my mentor to prayerfully ask God for a word and verse for this year. This year, my given word is "Hope." And the verse, "Let us hold unswervingly to the hope we profess, for he who promised is faithful" (Hebrews 10:23). This verse has been my guiding light throughout the year. I have meditated on this promise, talked about it, placed it where I look and God has helped me to believe in my heart that no matter what, He IS faithful in my life.

During loss, we need to reconnect with God through stopping and refocusing on the memory of our loved one and especially the memory of who Christ is and that we find our hope in Him.

Lord, being at the end of ourselves in turmoil brings us to our knees. As we come to your throne, please refresh our memories of your promises and goodness so we may be firmly established in your truth (2 Peter 1:12-13). Come, Lord Jesus, let your redeemed children tell their stories of love, care, loss, and redemption (Psalm 107:2). Amen.

♫ Find a Spotify Music Playlist for God of Reconnection at this link: www.goodmourningwithmarilyn.com/day3

Application

Read 2 Peter 1:12-13, what are we firmly established in? What is it right to do?

Let us remember who God is together. Read these Psalms displaying attributes of God. Write down any words that stand out to you.

Psalm 23:

Psalm 33:4-5:

Psalm 99:1-5:

Psalm 107:1-9:

Psalm 111:

Read John 14:26, ask God what truth about Him you need to recall right now. Put this truth wherever you may look, talk about it, and teach your mind with it.

What is one way God has redeemed you? What is one word or verse you can use to remember God's faithfulness?

What is your most treasured memory of your loved one? What "stones" will you place around you to remember?

Review the below list of ways to remember your loved one. Which one will you try this week?

☐ Talk about your loved one or even try talking to them.
☐ Pray about your love and loss.
☐ Draw, paint, sculpt or create something in remembrance of your loved one.
☐ Look at photos and write out cherished memories.
☐ Make a quilt with some of your loved one's clothing.
☐ Wear clothes or jewelry that reminds you of your loved one.
☐ Create a mask. Decorate the inside with how you feel. Decorate the outside with what you show the world on the outside of the mask.
☐ Cook a dish that your loved one enjoyed.
☐ Visit a restaurant you enjoyed with your loved one.
☐ Go to a place that reminds you of your loved one.
☐ Buy a bouquet of flowers that reminds you of your loved one. Display this bouquet in your home or workplace.
☐ Plant a tree, bush, or flowers in honor of your loved one. Create an outdoor plaque and rest near it.
☐ Run, walk, bike or support a charity race that has meaning to your type of loss.
☐ Watch movies that are centered around the theme of loss. How did the characters express their sadness? Do you feel this way too? I recommend children's films for this. They are simple and relatable, but not overwhelmingly emotional.
☐ Listen to music that reminds you of your love and loss (Refer to the Spotify Playlists in this devotional) Do you feel this way too? How did the musician express their sadness?
☐ Read stories of other survivors overcoming loss.
☐ Read or write your own poetry about loss.
☐ Visit the gravesite or memorial site.

DAY 4

GOD OF RENEWAL
Renew
My Identity

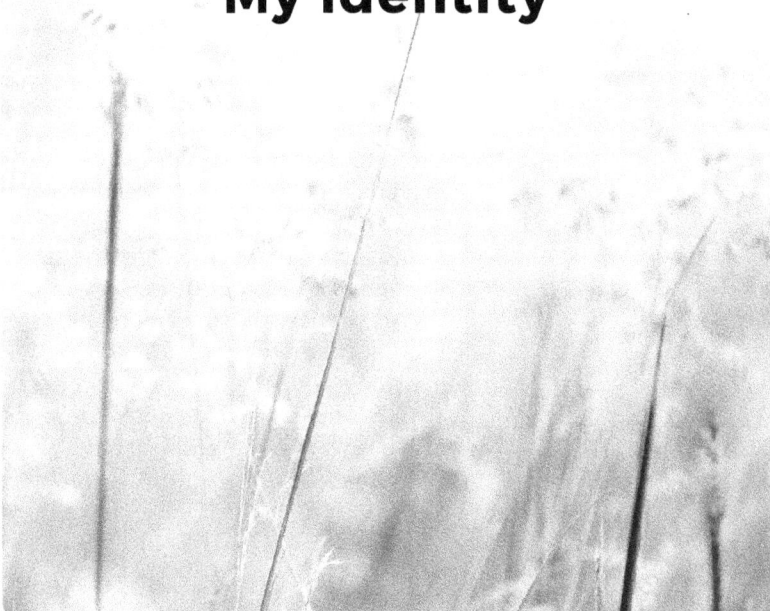

$\mathcal{D}ay\ 4$

?
Who am I now?
How do I put together my past, present, and future?
What does it look like to renew my identity?

**As you navigate loss,
your fourth need is for the
renewal of your identity
in Christ**

The primer is set; your chair is ready to be painted. While its foundation remains the same, the paint gives the chair a new appearance that is suited to the room. Much like we give a chair a new look, loss requires us to renew our Identity. We carry with us who we were before loss while adapting to our new reality. We practice this renewal by creating mental pictures of ourselves walking in a restored life. These pictures give us goals to strive towards – an end state to reaffirm.

God of Renewal

God is so gracious. From the very beginning, He had family in mind. We all know the story, God creates man and sees that he needs someone else, a companion. Then God makes a woman out of man and names this fitting partner. This first family unit reveals the close connection we all feel to our clan.

Names share with the world where we come from. The woman's name and physical body literally came out of "man." Later God uses the woman to be the giver of life creating a beautiful cycle where children physically come out of her body. Along with the child's physical body, a name is also given. Just like Adam and Eve, children begin life belonging to and in need of their parents. When we lose someone we consider family, we lose a part of the home, everyday connection, intimate knowing, and a place of belonging.

Names help us to remember who we are and where we belong (Luke 10:20).

- Abram's name was changed to Abraham meaning "the father of many nations." God promised that he and his barren wife would live up to his new names meaning (Genesis 17:5).

> "This is now bone of my bones and flesh of my flesh; she shall be called 'woman,' for she was taken out of man."
> (Genesis 2:23)

- Simon was given the name Peter, meaning "rock or stone." Simon's named changed when he revealed our messiah to us, the cornerstone of our faith, Jesus (Matthew 16:17).

- Jesus' mighty name means "to save." Jesus' name shares his purpose for coming to the world. He has the power to save by bringing eternal life through the forgiveness of sins. Jesus also saves us by healing us physically, spiritually, and emotionally (John 17:11) (John 4:42) (Acts 2:38) (Acts 3:6) (Acts 16:18).

God changes people's names in the Bible to show that they are now His and have a renewed purpose.

Similar to Abraham and Peter, our identity continues to renew when we accept Christ as our personal savior and are adopted into God's family (1 John 3:1) (John 1:12) (Revelation 21:7). Along with a new name, "child of God," we are invited to have both everlasting renewal and a renewed purpose (2 Corinthians 5:17).

"Yet to all who did receive him, to those who believed in his name, he gave the right to become children of God—"
(John 1:12)

"Those who are victorious will inherit all this, and I will be their God and they will be my children."
(Revelation 21:7)

"Therefore, if anyone is in Christ, the new creation has come: The old has gone, the new is here!"
(2 Corinthians 5:17)

"being confident of this, that he who began a good work in you will carry it on to completion until the day of Christ Jesus."
(Philippians 1:6)

Marilyn's Reflections

When I was in elementary school, I noticed that all of the women on both sides of my family had the middle name Catherine: my dad's mom, my mom's mom, and my mom. My mom's father tragically died while she was pregnant with me. Therefore, in his honor, I was named after him. Even at this young age, I recognized that I wanted to be a part of these women in my family. With my parent's blessing, we added Catherine to my middle name. The name our family gives us links us to them. When I look at my new name, I am reminded that I belong somewhere in this world.

Our identity will be first shaped by our earthly experiences. It continues to change when we accept Christ as our personal savior and are adopted into God's family (1 John 3:1) (John 1:12) (2 Corinthians 5:17) (Revelation 21:7). Upon adoption, the Holy Spirit will slowly move our fleshly identity in line with whom Christ created us to be (1 Corinthians 3:10-17) (1 Corinthians 9:27). This occurs slowly like peeling back layers of an onion (1 Corinthians 3:1-2). This transformation looks different for each of us, from Abram to Abraham, from Simon to Peter, from Marilyn Frances Jones to Marilyn Catherine Frances Willis.

Jesus promises that even though we outwardly waste away, He will inwardly renew us day by day (2 Corinthians 4:16-18). We lost a part of ourselves, someone whom we use to fit alongside. Many of us do not know what life is supposed to look like now. No matter how shattered our lives are, when we reconnect to God, He sustains us. He renews us. We are His (1 John 4:14) (John 4:42)!

> *No matter how shattered our lives are, when we reconnect to God, He sustains us. He renews us. We are His.*

Lord, as we think about renewing our identity many of us feel lost. It is hard to picture who we are and what life is without our loved ones. Please be our lamp and light our path ahead (2 Samuel 22:29). As we submit to your will, please send your gentle Holy Spirit to guide our steps each day (2 Corinthians 4:16-18). Please help us to renew our identity with Christ as our firm foundation, rock, and cornerstone (2 Corinthians 5:17) (2 Timothy 2:19). Amen.

Find a Spotify Music Playlist for God of Renewal at this link: www.goodmourningwithmarilyn.com/day4

Application

What healthy imprint on your identity have you received from your nuclear family? What healthy imprint have you received from the loved one who died?

Read John 1:12-13, what identity have you been given from receiving Christ?

Read Proverbs 3:3-4, what will win you favor and a good name in the sight of God and man?

How will your good name renew who you are and where you belong?

DAY **5**

GOD OF RESTORATION
For My Eternal Life

Day 5

"A restored me feels impossible."
"A new purpose feels impossible."
Once all seemed lost, but with God new life is found.

**As you navigate loss,
your fifth need is for a restored
meaning and purpose.**

It is now time to place that fully refurbished chair in your new room. A piece of furniture looks out of place if it does not appear purposeful and connect with the pieces of furniture around it. Likewise, in navigating loss we restore life after loss. "From your renewed identity comes a new life. Not a wholly different life, but a restored life that connects you to your purpose and calling. This new meaning and purpose solidifies what beauty remains in you and your life after loss. Ultimately restoring life after loss occurs through the reconnection with our story, God's bigger story, and the stories of others" (RESTORED, 2020).

God of Eternal Restoration

I am but a Breath

I seek you, Lord, creator of the world,
in my time of profound distress.
I know you gave it all for me,
the free gift of eternal life through my sin's
forgiveness
(Romans 6:23).

So why do I still long inside
and deal with so much strife?
Please Lord restore my heart and mind,
Lord to you I submit my life
(2 Corinthians 4:16).

While I remain here on earth
may I serve you well.
Let me point the world to You,
May Jesus' mercies
shine peace on those I tell
(Luke 1:78-79).

I know I am but a breath.
Lord, I need you more now than ever.
Restore my soul eternally
I long to be with you forever
(Ecclesiastes 7:2).

"For the wages of sin is death, but the gift of God is eternal life in Christ Jesus our Lord."
(Romans 6:23)

"Therefore we do not lose heart. Though outwardly we are wasting away, yet inwardly we are being renewed day by day."
(2 Corinthians 4:16)

"because of the tender mercy of our God, by which the rising sun will come to us from heaven to shine on those living in darkness and in the shadow of death, to guide our feet into the path of peace."
(Luke 1:78-79)

I know you are hurting. I wish I could take your pain away. Even though I do not have this power, I know the one who does. Let us look at the many ways Jesus restores our lives in eternity when we put our hope in Him. May He be present in your spirit as you read and reflect on these truths.

Lord, please restore our broken hearts and crushed spirits (Psalm 34:18)! My God of Order, may we trust you with our days and receive Your peace. My God of Comfort, may we mourn our losses and feel Your comfort so present. My God of Reconnection, may we know Your word and discover that Your promises bring us hope. My God of Renewal, may we recognize ourselves in You and be given Your unexplainable joy. My God of Restoration, may our souls find rest in You (Psalm 62). Amen.

♫♪ Find a Spotify Music Playlist for God of
Restoration at this link:
www.goodmourningwithmarilyn.com/day5

Application

Read Isaiah 61:3, what promises does this verse hold for you? Ask God that these promises will be true in your heart and life.

Read Isaiah 51:11, what promises are given here? Ask God that these promises will be true in your heart and life.

Read Revelation 21:4, what comfort do you gain from these verses? Ask God that these promises will be true in your heart and life.

Read 1 Thessalonians 4:15-18, what comfort do you gain from these verses? Ask God that these promises will be true in your heart and life.

Read Philippians 1:21-26, what does this verse tell us about God's purpose for life and death? What does this truth mean for you and your recent loss?

DAY **6**

GOD OF MY RESTORED MOMENTS

God of Current Restoration: Marilyn's Reflections

When I began my grief journey at fifteen years old, I could not wait for it to be "over." Like the cries of so many of God's people, I too was saying, "Lord, I am suffering. My heart is faint within me. Come, Lord Jesus, bring your comfort into my heart full of sorrow" (Jeremiah 8:18 NIV). Thank you, Father, that you are with me wherever I go, even into the depths of grief (Joshua 1:9 NIV). Please in your great mercy turn my tears into Your songs of joy. (Psalm 126:5 NIV) Amen.

> "Restore our fortunes, Lord, like streams in the Negev. Those who sow with tears will reap with songs of joy."
> (Psalm 126:4-5)

Now, over twenty years later, I hope for glimpses of grief to return.

My kids and I go on a daily adventure in our neighborhood. Bucket in hand, we are ready for the treasures we are sure to encounter. Three houses down the street, we must stop to take a quick plunge into the sprinklers. This always leads to laughter and playful squeals. Then the first rock is spotted – it is smooth and speckled, and after being inspected by my son, it is declared to be his, "favorite rock ever." Plunk! Into the bucket it goes. Then a green leaf is appreciated and placed gently into the bucket by my daughter. "We will examine this later," she tells me seriously. Once at a neighbor's house, my son picked a flower. It was the Rose of Sharon in full bloom. As his little hand reached out to offer the rose to me, his big blue eyes peered at me in expectation: "This is for you mommy. Just doing my job filling your bucket."

My spirit overflowed with joy as I was transported back in time remembering when my mom planted a Rose of Sharon in our backyard. She would snip off several of the flowers and put them in a vase, smiling at me as she placed it on the table. Mom was always finding ways to display beauty for all to enjoy.

Daily, my life is restored as my present and my past come together, colliding in memories, traditions, and legacies. As I heal, mom slowly becomes a special part of who I am. Mom's love continues through my memory; she calls to me.

Our lives are not restored all at once. Instead, they are renewed and restored day by day. Christ gives us our daily bread of hope through glimpses of His goodness in a sprinkler, a rock, and a leaf in a child's bucket. Christ's glory shines through His creation and calls to us.

These daily gifts beckon me to be more, to love more, to live more fully. Christ restores our current lives, our joy, through His gifts: His Rose of Sharon.

> Christ restores our current lives, our joy, through His gifts: His Rose of Sharon.

Application

What about your loved one beckons you to be more, live fully, and love tenderly? What is your "Rose of Sharon"?

What about Christ beckons you to be more, to love more, to live more fully. What gifts are inside your bucket?

What is one step you will take today toward restoring your current life?

It has truly been an honor to seek Christ with you. In closing I will share my earnest prayer of blessing over you:

When you are in need of order,
may Christ's sufficiency be tangible in your life (Romans 5:3).

When you are in need of comfort,
may Christ restore your strength and peace (2 Corinthians 12:10).

When you are in need of assurance,
may Christ remind you of His promises and faithfulness.

When you are in need of renewal,
may Christ remind you that you belong to Him.

As you navigate your loss,
may Christ grant you daily Restored Moments.

Amen.

Author Testimony

I grew up dyslexic. Mixing up the letters 'b' and 'd' was one of my largest challenges along with reading comprehension. To succeed in school, I had to overcompensate with organization, tedious highlighting, and a large dose of focus. If you would have told me that I would grow up to become an author I would have laughed and said there was a zero percent chance of that.
God had other plans.

My mom was the strongest woman I have ever known. She was diagnosed with cancer when I was twelve and never admitted defeat. Driven toward life until her last moment I thought she was invincible. I lost my mom when I was fifteen.
God had other plans.

I grew up in a Christian home, however, God became real to me in college. The Summer before my sophomore year I accepted Him into my heart. In the fall, I felt a leading to start a grief group on my campus. For the first time in my life, He showed up, after I stepped out in faith to lead this group. He shows up every time I step out in my weakness.

Out of my mom's death, God called me to counsel.
Out of a calling to help more people, God called me to write.

If we let Him, God uses each of our stories; the joyful and the hard moments, our strengths, and weaknesses our limitations, and resources, to shape our identity. God's plan is always different than we expect...often our best self is someone we never realized we were meant to be. Restoration has always looked different for me than I thought it would. My credentials make me laugh because they truly remind me of God's restoration.

To God be the glory!
Marilyn Willis, Award-Winning Author and Grief Counselor

If you are ready to further reconnect and walk towards restoration, my book "RESTORED: A Self-Paced Grief Workbook for Your Journey from Loss to Life," is a user-friendly grief workbook with practical steps for navigating the death of your loved one. Discover a step-by-step process to the restoration of body, mind, and spirit.

Order your copy today: www.goodmourningwithmarilyn.com/book

You don't have to face loss alone.

Move from loss to life with RESTORED: Your Journey from Loss to Life

Available everywhere books are sold.

Available at amazon   BARNES NOBLE

RESTORED
/ SELF-PACED GRIEF WORKBOOK FOR
YOUR JOURNEY FROM LOSS TO LIFE

MARILYN WI....

**Subscribe at
www.GoodMourningwithMarilyn.com
for more free grief resources.**

www.ingramcontent.com/pod-product-compliance
Lightning Source LLC
Chambersburg PA
CBHW071732020426
42331CB00008B/2003